Healthy Adventures

About This Book

- **Exciting Activities**: Engage kids with interactive and entertaining activities that make learning about nutrition fun.
- **Tasty Recipes**: Explore delicious and healthy recipes designed to encourage good food choices.
- **Family-Friendly:** Tailored for families, this book fosters a shared experience, encouraging discussions and activities together.
- **Promotes Healthy Habits:** Instill the importance of healthy living from a young age, laying the foundation for lifelong nutritious choices.
- **Inspired by Nutrition Knowledge:** Benefit from insights inspired by the author's background in food science, offering reliable and engaging information.
- **Designed for Ages 5-9:** Specifically crafted to captivate and educate young minds aged 5-9, making it age-appropriate and enjoyable.

After Reading

After exploring the 'Healthy Eating Adventure,' let's turn these lessons into daily habits! Encourage your young reader to make nutritious choices, have fun in the kitchen, and embrace a healthy lifestyle. The adventure continues in their daily lives, promoting a lifelong journey of well-being!"

Design & Presented By

Calmly Productions

Inside the book

What is Nutrition?

Nutrition is all about the food you eat and how it helps your body. It's like a secret code in your food that gives you vitamins, protein, and other things that help you grow and stay healthy. Eating different foods like fruits, veggies, milk, and grains is like collecting superpowers that make you strong and happy.

Benefits of Vegetables

- **Colorful Magic:** Veggies come in many colors like red, green, and orange, each color gives your body special magic to stay healthy.
- **Brainy Foods:** Eating veggies helps your brain think better and makes it easier to learn new things in school.
- **Strong Bones:** Veggies make your bones and muscles strong, making it easier to run and play your favorite games.
- **Happy Tummy:** They help your tummy feel good and help you avoid getting sick, so you can have more fun with friends and family.
- **Energy Powerhouse:** Veggies give you the power to be a sports star, making it easier to run fast, jump high, and play your favorite games!
- **Vitamin Magic:** Eating vegetables helps your body get special vitamins that keep you healthy and make you strong.
- **Growth Fuel:** Veggies help you grow taller and keep your body working well.
- **Energy Boost:** They give you the power you need to run, jump, and have lots of fun during the day.

Yummy Cheesy Broccoli Bites

You've probably seen broccoli bites in the freezer section, but did you know you can make them at home? It's so easy! Just blend some ingredients, shape them into bites, and bake. simple ingredients to make this delicious meal for little ones at home.

Ingredients:

- Fully boiled potatoes
- 1 Egg
- Fresh or frozen broccoli
- Shredded cheese (any kind you like)
- Breadcrumbs (plain or gluten-free)

Tempreture: 180c for 15-20 min
180° C is equivalent to 356° F

Recipe: Cheesy Broccoli Bites

Step-by-Step Instructions:

Prepare Broccoli:
- Chop the broccoli into small pieces.
- Pour hot water over the broccoli and let it sit to soften.
- Drain the broccoli well.

Blend Ingredients:
- In a food processor, combine the boiled potatoes, softened broccoli, egg, shredded cheese, and breadcrumbs.
- Blend until you get a uniform batter.

Shape into Bites:
- Preheat your oven to the temperature recommended for baking.
- Using a tablespoon, scoop out portions of the batter and shape them into bite-sized.

Bake:
- Place the shaped bites onto a parchment-lined baking sheet.
- Bake in the preheated oven according to the recommended time or until the bites are golden and cooked through.

Enjoy Warm:
- Once baked, let the bites cool for a bit before serving.
- These broccoli bites are delicious when warm.

Dip and Enjoy:
- Serve the bites with ketchup or ranch for a tasty dip.
- Try dipping them and discover your favorite way to enjoy these yummy broccoli bites!

MATCH THE PARTS

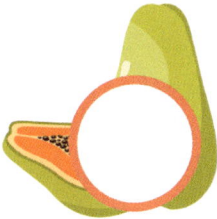

HELP THE LITTLE HEDGEHOG FIND THE WAY TO THE APPLE

Write the Answer here

_____

FIND TWO THE SAME PICTURES

ANSWER

?

Yummy Carrot Cake

Healthy Carrot Cake

50 gr Honey

200gr Nuts

8gr Sea Salt

8gr Olive Oil

1 Egg

3 Grated Carrots

350gr Almond Milk

Mix Everything

Spread in a container and let it rest for 2 hours

Bake the cake for 25 min at 220°C

For cake topping, mix 50gr coconut flour and 200gr Greek yogurt

Spread the Topping in the cake surface and serve...

... and Bon Appétit!

Spell it Out!

p g a
lg e n t

Benefits of fruits

Including a mix of colorful fruits in a child's diet brings lots of benefits and keeps them healthy and happy!

Benefits

Growth Helpers: Fruits have vitamins and minerals that help kids grow strong.

Quick Energy: Eating fruits gives a quick and healthy energy boost, perfect for playtime.

Happy Tummies: Fruits with fiber keep tummies healthy and help with pooping easily.

Strong Immunity: Fruits, like oranges, make the body strong to fight off sickness.

Stay Hydrated: Many fruits have water, keeping kids refreshed, especially on warm days.

Strong Bones: Some fruits, like oranges, help make bones strong and healthy.

Healthy Snacking: Fruits are yummy snacks that are good for the body and don't make you too full.

Better Focus: Eating fruits helps kids concentrate better, especially during school or fun activities.

Good Habits: Eating different fruits helps kids learn to like healthy foods from a young age.

BERRY SMOOTHIE

1 Cup raspberries or blackberries
1 Cup blueberries
1/2 Cup vanilla yogurt
1/2 Cup frozen strawberries
1 Cup sliced bananas
1/2 Cup
2-3 ice cubes
Mix until smooth and top it with some raspberries and a
blueberry in the middle enjoy!

Arrange the Letters in Order

 **amoott** _____

 **cheyrr** _____

 **oacrrt** _____

 **librccoo** _____

CROSSWORD FOR KIDS

C
A P
O
S W
B
L

How Many?

COUNT THE SIMILAR FRUIT AND WRITE THE NUMBER

WORD PUZZLE GAME

R	C	H	Q	S	D	L	E	W	Y
H	J	Z	J	G	E	O	G	A	R
D	C	Q	U	O	P	I	G	T	R
Q	R	F	S	E	P	P	E	E	E
M	M	D	S	K	O	E	G	R	B
A	N	A	C	Z	T	A	N	M	W
P	S	S	N	I	A	R	A	E	A
P	A	L	J	G	M	R	R	L	R
L	A	N	A	C	O	T	O	O	T
E	M	E	V	O	T	A	U	N	S

- orange - pear - apple - mango - tomato - watermelon - strawberry -

Banana Bread Easy Recipe

BANANA BREAD

125 G OF BUTTER

1 TSP OF BAKING POWDER

1 1/2 CUPS OF SUGAR

1 TSP OF BAKING SODA

1 1/2 CUPS OF FLOUR

1 TSP OF VANILLA ESSENCE

2 EGSS

CHOCOLATE CHIPS

3 RIPE BANANAS

1/2 CUP OF NATURAL YOGURT

HOW TO

- PRE-HEAT TO 180° C
- MIX WET INGREDIENTS
- MIX DRY INGREDIENTS
- POUR IN A LOAF TIN
- BAKE FOR 40 MIN

Balanced Eating

Fruits and veggies are like the colorful superheroes of our meals, but Our bodies also need other special foods:

- **Dairy Products:** These, like milk and cheese, give us strong bones and teeth, making us grow big and tall.
- **Meat:** It has super proteins that help muscles become strong, like the muscles of our favorite action heroes.
- **Eggs:** Eggs are like nature's own superheroes, packed with nutrients that help us grow and stay healthy.
- **Nuts:** These are tiny but powerful snacks that give us energy and keep our brains super smart.
- **Exercise:** Just like superheroes need to move and play, our bodies love exercise! Running, jumping, and playing sports make our muscles strong, our hearts happy, and our minds super sharp.

So, by eating a bit of everything – fruits, veggies, dairy products, meat, eggs, and nuts – and having lots of fun with exercise, we make our bodies happy and strong! It's like having a team of different superheroes in our meals and activities.

Hi there! I'm passionate about helping kids aged 5-9 learn about healthy eating through fun activities, tasty recipes, and cool food facts. Studying food science showed me how crucial good nutrition is for a healthy life. This adventure is my way of making learning about healthy choices exciting. Our small family team, including my two awesome daughters, is dedicated to creating a guide full of activities, recipes, and food knowledge to inspire healthy habits. Your support means a lot! Your reviews help us keep creating fun and informative content. We'd love to hear about your experience with our Healthy Eating Adventure. Thanks for joining us on this journey to a healthier and happier life!

Made in the USA
Las Vegas, NV
11 April 2024